THE IMPENDING GLEAM

Glen Baxter

FONTANA/COLLINS

To my parents

First published in Great Britain by Jonathan Cape Ltd 1981
First issued in Fontana Paperbacks 1983

Copyright © Glen Baxter 1981

Made and printed in Great Britain by
William Collins Sons & Co. Ltd., Glasgow

Many of the drawings in this book are
in private and public collections,
including those of the Arts Council of Great Britain
and the Victoria and Albert Museum.

CONTENTS

Way out West

From the Pages of History

The Trouble at St. Mildred's

The Shadow over Dringfield

PECOS BILL HAD A "THING"
ABOUT HOUSEHOLD DUST...

YOUNG ERIC HAD PREPARED HIMSELF FOR
ALMOST ANY EMERGENCY....

"I'VE CALLED ABOUT THE POST OF
ASSISTANT MILLINER" DRAWLED DEKE

" I PRUNE MY CHRYSANTHEMUMS THIS-A-WAY..."

Professions of the Old West

No. 2

The Dentist

"TO ME THE WINDOW IS STILL
A SYMBOLICALLY LOADED MOTIF"
DRAWLED CODY

"I MAKE A LIVING PEDDLING DANDRUFF"
SNORTED THE OLD TIMER

"SO YOU SEE, BOYS— WHAT A PICTURE MUST HAVE
IN COMMON WITH REALITY, IN ORDER TO BE
ABLE TO DEPICT IT — CORRECTLY OR INCORRECTLY
— IN THE WAY IT DOES, IS ITS PICTORIAL FORM"
EXPLAINED TEX

PANCHO'S SLEEPING ARRANGEMENTS WERE THE TALK
OF THE BUNKHOUSE

JEDSON WAS NOTED FOR HIS WITHERING
SIDELONG GLANCES

IT WAS TOM'S FIRST BRUSH WITH MODERNISM

"THE WAY I FIGGER IT — TRUTH IS UN-TRUTH INSOFAR AS THERE BELONGS TO IT THE RESERVOIR OF THE NOT-YET-REVEALED, THE UN-UNCOVERED IN THE SENSE OF CONCEALMENT" REASONED McTAGGART.

IT WAS THE HALITOSIS KID.....

"I KEEP MY BAGELS IN HERE" WHISPERED
THE DESPERADO

"I STUB MY CIGARS OUT.......THERE!"
SNORTED THE TEXAN

HE WAS FORCED TO ENDURE TERRIBLE
IMPERSONATIONS OF CATHY McGOWAN

YOUNG HANK ENTERTAINED THE BOYS
WITH A FINE DISPLAY OF SMOULDERING

AT THE GIVEN SIGNAL, MRS BOTHAM
POPPED OUT FROM THE CONCEALED
LINING AND BLASTED THE RATTLER

WILD BILL WAS KNOWN TO GO TO
EXTRAORDINARY LENGTHS TO CATCH
"THE LUCY SHOW" REPEATS ON CHANNEL 6

VANCE LIVED IN CONSTANT FEAR
OF LOSING HIS WRISTWATCH....

McGUIRE SEEMED TO HAVE RIDDEN INTO A
TRAP.....

THE LOMAX BOYS KEPT UP AN ALL-NIGHT
VIGIL ON THE NOUGAT

SETH TOOK HIS TEA AT SEVEN ON THE DOT

BIG JEB WAS A TRICKY CUSTOMER
ALLRIGHT

FRUITS OF THE WORLD
IN
DANGER

Number 10   The Apricot

"BUT SURELY, LANGUAGE IS NOT
DEFINED FOR US AS AN ARRANGE
-MENT FULFILLING A DEFINITE
PURPOSE..." STAMMERED JED.

HOW HE HATED SATURDAY MORNING SHOPPING

GREAT
MOMENTS
IN HISTORY
Number 43
The First Omelette

IT WAS A MONDAY AFTERNOON JUST LIKE
ANY OTHER.......

From the Pages of History

IT WAS A SMALL VOTIVE BUST
OF HELEN SHAPIRO.....

IT WAS THE SMALLEST PIZZA THEY HAD
EVER SEEN

"NOT SO FAST, VARLET — I DEMAND A SECOND FITTING!" BELLOWED SIR PEREGRINE

ROBIN WAS CERTAINLY IMPRESSED
WITH THE SIMULATED TEAK FINISH

YOUNG ARTHUR'S EARRINGS WERE
THE TALK OF NOTTINGHAM

FRUITS OF THE WORLD
IN
DANGER

Number 12 The Kumquat

SIR ROLAND TRIED TO CONVINCE THE
SCEPTICS OF THE POTENTIAL OF HIS
LIGHTWEIGHT "MINI-SHIELD".......

"WHAT HAVE YOU DONE WITH MY WIMPLE?"
GROWLED BIG 'BULL' HARPER

GREAT FAILURES OF OUR TIME

Nº 16
The First Yo-Yo

IT WAS HUNGARIAN COOKING
ALLRIGHT.....

IT WAS HORRIBLE. FROM MY VANTAGE POINT 1 COULD
SEE THE STRUGGLING FIGURES BEING CARTED INTO
PROFESSOR TREMBO'S STRUCTURALIST FILM SEMINAR

HE TOOK HER IN HIS ARMS AND
GENTLY SQUEEZED HER GOATEE

" AH YES, MR. WRIGGLESWORTH — IT'S ABOUT THIS.... AHEM.... FIRST DRAFT OF YOUR NOVEL" SPLUTTERED MR. SCELPE

THE TWO MEN WERE IN AGREEMENT
— IT WAS A WORK OF SOME MERIT

THE TWO MEN WERE IN AGREEMENT
—IT WAS A WORK WITHOUT MERIT

FRUITS OF THE WORLD
IN
DANGER

Number 1   The Orange

"I SENSED THAT BRENDA WAS TRYING
TO IMPRESS ME....."

AFTER TEA, MONICA WAS FORCED TO ENACT
THE GRIM RITUAL OF "COUNTING THE STUMPS"

DEIDRE POINTED OUT HER SUPPLY OF HASHISH
FOR THE AUTUMN TERM

ANGELA ADDRESSED THE MEMBERS OF
THE CROCHET CLUB ON HER PROPOSALS
FOR DEALING WITH LATECOMERS

MISS FROBISHER MADE A POINT OF
THREATENING NEW ARRIVALS WITH
"THE NOSE TWEAKER"

MIRANDA HAD STUMBLED UPON OUR
SUPPLY OF BEARDS.....

IT HAD BEEN SUSPECTED FOR SOME TIME
THAT MAVIS WAS EXPERIMENTING WITH A
COMBINATION OF BALKAN AND TURKISH BLENDS

DAPHNE BEGAN TO SENSE SHE WAS NO
LONGER ALONE.......

"GOING DOWN TO THE VILLAGE
AGAIN, EH?" SNAPPED MADGE

BERYL HAD HIT UPON A WAY OF RELIEVING
THE TEDIUM OF MISS ABERGHAST'S LESSONS

HE WAS FROM BROOKLYN ALLRIGHT

GREAT FAILURES
OF OUR TIME
№ 160

The First Pencil Sharpener

"SO YOU'RE THE MYOPIC MULDONI BOYS FROM CHICAGO, EH?" SPAT LANNIGAN

THE NURSE ENTERED WITH THE
BRIGADIER'S CALORIE—CONTROLLED
BREAKFAST....

GUSTAV'S NEON WIMPLE WAS CLEARLY
FAILING TO IMPRESS THELMA

"SOME ARE HAM AND SOME ARE CHEESE AND PICKLE" CONFIDED PANDOWSKI

"I SUPPOSE YOU'RE ALL WONDERING WHY I'VE
GATHERED YOU HERE TODAY" WHISPERED THE BOSUN

IT WAS THE FOURTH TIME THAT DADDY HAD FALLEN FOR THE EXPLODING FORK ROUTINE...

THERE WAS A HINT OF TRIUMPH
IN UNCLE FRANK'S BLUE EYES

THERE WAS GENUINE CONCERN IN
DAPHNE'S FRANK BLUE EYES

HE WAS NOT THE MAN SHE
HAD LOVED THAT EVENING
IN BRIDGEPORT......

The Shadow
over
Dringfield

"I HOPE YOU CAN EXPLAIN THAT MOUND
OF PEANUT HUSKS IN MY BEDROOM!"
SNAPPED GATTING

"THERE'S ONLY ONE WAY TO
EAT WHELKS" HISSED GREIG

THE LADS HAD A WAY OF DEALING
WITH BORING OLD RELATIVES

"I'M AFRAID IT'S GRIM NEWS, SANDY—
THE VICE-CONSUL INTENDS TO BAN
THE WEARING OF WIMPLES AFTER 7-15 P.M"

"WHEN THIS IS SWITCHED ON, YOUR
PANTS WILL BE CLEANED AND PRESSED
EVERY TWO MINUTES" SNAPPED TOWLE

SUNDAYS CAME AROUND WITH
DEPRESSING REGULARITY

THERE WAS STILL MUCH TO
LEARN ABOUT SZECHUAN
CUISINE.....

IT WAS A DEVICE FOR TURNING SCHOOL MEALS
BACK INTO FOOD

" IF THERE HAS BEEN A MISHAP ON THE
SPORTS FIELD THEN NATURALLY I WANT TO
BE THE FIRST TO KNOW " MUMBLED THE
HEADMASTER

WITH AN AIR OF WEARIED RESIGNATION
PROFESSOR COOMBES TUCKED THE ESSAY
BACK INTO MY BEARD

HE HAD BEEN CAUGHT USING THE
FORBIDDEN "HEAD-PEN" AGAIN.....

"BUT ...... I ... ORDERED THE
CHICKEN KIEV..." BLURTED COOPER

"I'LL THANK YOU TO STOP JUGGLING MY GHERKINS!"
SNORTED THE ANGUISHED THROGUE

"NOW WHICH ONE OF YOU IS MRS. BLOYARD?"
ASKED THE INSPECTOR

BARTWELL SAW THROUGH THE DISGUISE
ALMOST IMMEDIATELY

HAMMOND OUTLINED THE RUDIMENTS
OF HIS DARING ESCAPE PLAN

ESSENTIAL SUPPLIES WERE DROPPED
TO THE BRITISH AGENTS....